# HENRY WADSWORTH LONGFELLOW

## AMERICAN POET, LINGUIST, AND EDUCATOR

The Library of American Thinkers™

# HENRY WADSWORTH LONGFELLOW

## AMERICAN POET, LINGUIST, AND EDUCATOR

Meghan Fitzmaurice

rosen central™

The Rosen Publishing Group, Inc., New York

Published in 2006 by The Rosen Publishing Group, Inc.
29 East 21st Street, New York, NY 10010

First Edition

**Library of Congress Cataloging-in-Publication Data**

Fitzmaurice, Meghan.
Henry Wadsworth Longfellow: American poet, linguist, and educator/Meghan Fitzmaurice.
    p. cm.–(The library of American thinkers)
Includes bibliographical references and index.
ISBN 1-4042-0503-9 (library binding)
1. Longfellow, Henry Wadsworth, 1807–1882. 2. Poets, American–19th century–
Biography. I. Title. II. Series.

PS2281.F58 2005
811'.3–dc22

                                                                          2005013604

*Printed in China*

**On the cover:** Inset: Henry Wadsworth Longfellow, circa 1878. Background: A painting titled *Paul Revere's Midnight Ride* (artist unknown).

# CONTENTS

# INTRODUCTION

*A single conversation across the table with a wise man is better than ten years' mere study of books.*

—Henry Wadsworth Longfellow

L iterary scholars often refer to the decades of the nineteenth century leading up to the American Civil War—in particular the years from 1840 to 1865—as the American Renaissance. During this time, a group of remarkable poets, novelists, and thinkers—Walt Whitman, Herman Melville, Emily Dickinson, Nathaniel Hawthorne, Edgar Allan Poe, Henry David Thoreau, and Ralph Waldo Emerson—created a body of work that could stand on its own as a distinctly American literature.

As a young nation so newly independent, the United States could sometimes be unsure of itself with regard to older, more established nations, particularly those of Europe. England, primarily, but also France and Spain had controlled what was now American territory within the previous century. Even the Netherlands' colonial rule over New Amsterdam (New York) had ended less than 200 years previously. Even more so than today, the United States in the nineteenth century was a nation of immigrants. In 1850, a little more than 2.2 million Americans—almost 10 percent of the U.S. population—were born in foreign countries. That number rose to more than 13 percent of the population by 1860, and it remained between 13 and 15 percent until the 1920s, when it began a steady decline that has only been reversed in the past thirty years or so.

Today, those numbers are approaching nineteenth-century levels, with more than 33 million people in the United States having been born elsewhere. That is approximately 12 percent of the population. Today, however, the majority of that foreign-born population—more than two-thirds—is from Asia or Latin America. In the nineteenth century, most of that immigrant population—90 percent—was from Europe. In the first half of the nineteenth century, most of these European immigrants were from three countries: Great Britain, France, and Germany. (A tremendous amount of those listed as being from Great Britain, especially after 1840, were in fact from Ireland, which Britain then ruled as a colonial possession.)

You will sometimes hear people express fear and concern over the number of immigrants in the United States. They

The American artist Samuel Waugh painted this scene of Irish immigrants disembarking in New York City, entitled *The Bay and Harbor of New York*, in 1847. That year is remembered in Irish history as "Black '47," the worst year of the great Irish potato famine. Some of Ireland's tragedy was America's gain; over the next several years, poverty and hunger drove hundreds of thousands of Irish to immigrate to the United States.

argue that these new immigrants, with their origins in Latin America and Asia, will somehow not be able to assimilate in the same way that the earlier immigrants did. Because they do not share the European roots of American culture, the argument goes, they are essentially less deserving of becoming American citizens. They are believed to be less likely to understand, appreciate, and partake in American culture.

Similar concerns were expressed about immigration in the nineteenth century in the United States, particularly after 1850, when Irish and southern and eastern Europeans replaced the English and the Germans as the largest immigrant groups. Intense concern was expressed that these newcomers were so culturally different from other Americans that they would never be able to mix fully in American society. An equal concern was that their great numbers meant that their own cultural practices might overwhelm and replace American traditions.

The point behind this historical digression is to indicate that there was and is still evidence that the United States as a society shows a significant degree of insecurity about its identity. It is both proud of its history as a nation of immigrants and, throughout that history, fearful of the ways in which those immigrants might shape its identity. One can safely say that Americans have a very complex set of attitudes and beliefs regarding the foreign homelands from which they and their ancestors, and their neighbors and their ancestors descend.

There are fundamental questions at issue in this matter of identity: What is an American? Does one have to be born an American, or is it something one can become? Who is an American? How does one become one? If anyone, from any background, can become an American, then what does it mean to be one? How is it special or different? It is important to remember that even today some countries, such as Germany, still have a primarily "blood" standard of who can achieve the full measure of citizenship. Other countries, such as Israel, base citizenship on the ability to prove one's standing as the member of a particular ethnic, cultural, or religious group.

Today, questions about American identity are answered against the backdrop of the more than 200 years of history of the United States as a free nation. There is therefore an

"American experience" that informs any notion of an individual or shared American identity. The United States' growth as a world power, as well as its continued status as a golden or promised land for immigrants, means that this American experience is one that is also shared, in part, by many of the world's non-American residents. For better or worse, there is also little doubt today that there is an American culture. Indeed, the military and economic power and influence of the United States today is so great that for many people of other nations, the question of how to keep American culture from pervading and overwhelming their own is a very real issue.

But in the early decades of the nineteenth century (up until the Civil War, at which point America's conception of itself changed radically), these questions of American identity and culture were experienced very differently by Americans. Nineteenth-century Americans were extremely proud of the American Revolution (1775–1783) and the status it had given the United States as the world's only true republic. In the very first paragraph of the first Federalist Paper, for example, written in late 1787, Alexander Hamilton wrote that should the movement to establish a constitution for the United States fail, it should be considered as nothing less than the "general misfortune of mankind."

But Americans wondered what else would distinguish America as a society and a culture. They were less sure that their democracy would create a society of great cultural and intellectual distinction. Americans were fond of looking to the great civilizations of ancient Greece and Rome as models and inspiration for their political life. But they wondered whether the civilization they were creating would ever be able to compare or last in the same way. After all, ancient Greece and Rome had established cultures that had influenced Western civilization for thousands of years. Could young America establish itself in the same way? Speaking at Harvard University in 1837, in the famous address that would become known as "The American Scholar," Ralph Waldo Emerson, the foremost American intellectual of the day, expressed his hope that "perhaps the time is already come . . . when the sluggard intellect of this continent [i.e. North America, specifically the United States] will look from under its iron lids and fill the postponed expectation of the world with something better than the exertions of mechanical skill. Our day of dependence, our long apprenticeship to the learning of other lands, draws to a close."

In looking at Europe, Americans took great pride in their country's newness, its vitality and energy, and its opportunity. That newness was also cause for wonder, for it seemed America had so little with which to build a new, distinctly American culture. Its history, after all, was so brief; its people so newly removed from other homelands; its shared experience still too new to give rise to the distinctive myths, legends, stories, and traditions that define a culture. The languages Americans spoke were European languages, their religions were European religions, the people–many of them, anyway–were still in some ways European. Just as rich Americans imported their luxuries and fineries from Europe, sophisticated Americans looked to Europe for culture.

Alexis de Tocqueville (1805–1859) was a young French nobleman who visited the United States in 1831 for the purpose of examining the kind of society that democracy was creating. The result of his trip, *Democracy in America*, published in two volumes in 1835 and 1840, has been called by the historians Harvey Mansfield and Delba Winthrop (in their introduction to the 2000 edition of the book) "at once the best book ever written on democracy and the best book ever written on America." Few historians or literary critics would argue with this evaluation.

During his visit to the United States, Tocqueville observed that "when one enters the shop of a bookseller in the United States and inspects the American books that fill the shelves," one is struck by the fact that "most of these works have been composed in Europe. The Americans reprint them, adapting them to their use." Tocqueville concluded that

> although America is perhaps the civilized country of
> our day where people are least occupied by literature,
> one nevertheless meets a great quantity of individuals
> there who are interested in things of the mind . . .

HERE AND THERE;
Or, Emigration a Remedy.

This 1850 engraving from the English humor magazine *Punch*, entitled "Here and There; Or, Emigration a Remedy," depicts the alleged improvements to be enjoyed by the United Kingdom's poor if they immigrated to the United States. Many foreign governments viewed the economic opportunity presented by the United States as a solution to the problem of poverty in their own countries.

But England furnishes them most of the books they demand. Almost all of the great English works are reproduced in the United States. The literary genius of Great Britain casts its rays deep in the forests of the New World. There is scarcely a pioneer's cabin where one does not encounter some volumes of Shakespeare . . .

Not only do Americans draw every day on treasures from English literature, but one can truthfully say that they find the literature of England on their own soil. Among the few men in the United States who are occupied in composing works of literature, most are English at bottom and above all in form. Thus they transport into the midst of democracy the ideas and literary usages that are current in the aristocratic nation they have taken for a model. They paint with colors borrowed from foreign mores; almost never representing in its reality the country that has seen them born, they are rarely popular there.

Citizens of the United States themselves seem so convinced that books are not published for them, that before settling on the merit of one of their writers, they ordinarily wait for him to have been sampled in England . . .

The inhabitants of the United States, therefore, still do not have a literature, properly speaking.

Most American intellectuals would have agreed with Tocqueville. It seemed that although America had obtained its political independence, it remained an economic and cultural colony of England and other European countries. It seemed so to Europeans as well. With political men of genius, the Americans were abundantly blessed: Benjamin Franklin, Thomas Jefferson, and George Washington, in particular, were well known in Europe and even revered in many places as symbols of liberty. But who were the great American writers? Where were the great poems, novels, and plays? Where were the great American universities? Why were there no great American composers? Where were the great American opera houses and theaters? Some doubted that America even had the raw material from which to develop a vital, real culture. They thought it was an undisciplined, uneducated, polyglot land of overenergetic, grasping merchants, restless artisans (mechanics), rude backwoodsmen, zealous religious dissenters, imperious plantation owners, struggling small farmers, captive black chattel slaves, and soon-to-be-extinct native "savages"— not the stuff from which "real" culture was made. The best that could develop from such a democratic mix, such thinking held, was a coarse, popular, "low" culture, not anything that could ever stand up to the great achievements of the Europeans.

For figures such as Emerson, however, it was America's democratic culture, with its lack of inherited privilege and absence of an aristocratic ruling class, that afforded it the opportunity to make its own great literature. Emerson argued in "The American Scholar," that the American Revolution had brought power and rights to those who had never before had a voice in government, and the society created by the Revolution was still in the process of defining itself. This new society could create a literature in which those who had been previously silent would now have a voice. New subjects could be

John Whetten Ettinger depicted this scene of nineteenth-century American life, entitled *Yankee Peddler*, in 1853. New England intellectuals such as Ralph Waldo Emerson, Henry David Thoreau, Herman Melville, Nathaniel Hawthorne, and Henry Wadsworth Longfellow believed that everyday American life could serve as inspiration for and be the subject of authentic American literature.

explored. As Emerson put it, "the same movement which affected the elevation of what was called the lowest class in the state, assumed in literature a very marked and as benign an aspect . . . the near, the low, the common [could be] explored and poetized." In democratic America, Emerson proudly observed "the literature of the poor, the feelings of the child, the philosophy of the street, the meaning of household life, are the topics of the time—and fit subjects for literature."

It is in this context that the work of the writers mentioned in the first paragraph of this introduction remains so important. In taking to heart Emerson's warning that "we have listened too long to the courtly muses of Europe," these writers accepted Emerson's challenge to create a distinctly American literature, born out of the American experience and reflecting American sensibilities. In so doing, they helped create, define, and explain the American character. But the high regard that Emerson, Whitman, Thoreau, Hawthorne, Poe, Dickinson, and Melville enjoy today is not reflective of their stature during their own lifetimes. Of those seven, only Emerson and perhaps Hawthorne can be said to have enjoyed respect and recognition in their own time at all equal to their literary achievements. Even the idea that their life and work amounted to an "American Renaissance" is a modern notion. That term was not coined in reference to them until 1941, by the literary scholar F. O. Matthiessen. Most of these figures were judged failures in their own lifetimes.

Surprisingly, perhaps, the writer who was internationally regarded as being the most successful in creating a true American literature is almost never discussed in that context today. The poet Henry Wadsworth Longfellow is remembered, if he is remembered at all, as a "minor" poet, best suited to be read by children. But in the years between 1840 and his death in 1882, it was Longfellow, by far, who was the most successful, most acclaimed, and most revered American writer, in the United States as well as in Europe. He was lionized on both continents, and American and European literary figures considered it their duty to make a pilgrimage to his famous home in Cambridge, Massachusetts. There, he numbered among his friends and admirers some of the most important literary, scientific, intellectual, and political men of the day. This list includes Emerson, the scientist Louis Agassiz, the historians Francis Parkman and William Prescott, and the abolitionist Charles Sumner.

Longfellow did more than just awaken his fellow countrymen and Europeans to the potential of American literature. As an educator, Longfellow was largely responsible for introducing Americans to some of the glorious works of European literature that had gone overlooked in his country, especially the work of Dante Alighieri and Johann Wolfgang von Goethe. He was also a pioneer in teaching modern foreign languages in the United States. As his most recent biographer Charles C. Calhoun points out, Longfellow "would have been astonished that Americans can graduate from college and think themselves educated without being able to read one or more foreign languages." Longfellow himself was fluent in Spanish, German, French, and Italian and could read at least six more modern foreign tongues as well as Latin, ancient Greek, and Norse.

The first authoritative critical study of Longfellow, *American Prosody* by G. W. Allen, published in 1935, includes a quote from Longfellow that the "chief end of poetry is to give delight, to build an ideal world of 'escape' from a realistic world, and, finally, to honor God." This insistence may make Longfellow seem unfashionably sentimental and old-fashioned to some people today. For example, the much-honored contemporary American poet Stanley Kunitz, in an interview for a September 2000 Associated Press article entitled "Longfellow's Home, Reputation Rehabilitated," derides Longfellow's work because in it "there is no deep soul-searching, no probing of the inner life and no glory of language. It's a rhyming art at a somewhat prosaic level."

However, such criticism deliberately ignores what Longfellow was trying to achieve with his poetry. "His poems," according to the modern American poet Richard Howard in the September 2000 Associated Press article, "were consciously aimed at a general audience, a newly literate public that wanted to hear stories about America and wanted to be given popular myths." In that sense, Longfellow was well ahead of his time. In a recent exhibit, the Maine Historical Society characterized Longfellow as the "man who invented America." That may be somewhat of an exaggeration, but Longfellow's patriotic belief that the American experience could create a literature as great as the new American political system and society, as well as his conviction that great literature is a necessity for any great nation, makes him someone well worth remembering.

# CHAPTER
# 1

# "THE HEART'S DEEP HISTORY"

To outsiders, there was something blessed and charmed about the house and the liveliness that went on inside it. It was hard to imagine unhappiness even stopping there. It was as if the house, as well as its inhabitants, were invested with the same good fortune that had blessed the young country since those bold days when it had dared to declare its independence.

It had been built in 1759, a large, two-story Georgian structure, now painted yellow with white trim, with two huge fireplaces within, four white pillars without, two patios ("piazzas" in the New England

This famous photograph of the poet Henry Wadsworth Longfellow was taken on the Isle of Wight in 1868 by Julia Margaret Cameron. She is considered today to be one of the great photographic pioneers. Cameron's methods and the technology available to her required her subjects to sit still for a long time, and she could be very demanding of her subjects. The British poet laureate Alfred Lord Tennyson brought Longfellow to his sitting with Cameron, leaving him with the words, "Longfellow, you will have to do whatever she tells you. I shall return soon and see what is left of you."

parlance of the day) flanking its east and west wings, and a widow's walk atop. (A widow's walk is a railed observation platform on the roof of a house in a coastal area. It was originally built for the purpose of allowing the woman of the house to look for some distance out at sea for the sails of the ship bearing her seafaring husband or sons home. The failure of many men to return home safely is why the platform became known as the widow's walk.) The house stood about a half-mile outside of what was then the village of Cambridge, Massachusetts. A broad, green meadow, home to rabbits, salamanders, songbirds, and frogs, ran from the house's front steps to the Charles River.

## A HOUSE RICH IN HISTORY

The house exuded comfort and wealth. John Vassall, a rich Boston merchant, had built it as a country retreat for his family. It kept company in the area with similar homes, built by similarly prosperous Boston merchants. As the American Revolution approached, these country retreats became an increasingly welcome refuge for these men and their families, whose success in business inclined them toward loyalty to Great Britain and thus made them anxious to escape the tumult in rebellious Boston. The area became known as something of a Loyalist enclave and was often referred to as Tory Row. ("Tory" was an informal term used in the American colonies to

Few American houses have been home to as much history as this pale-yellow structure. The Craigie House, as it came to be known, was the first headquarters of commander in chief George Washington during the American Revolution and later was the residence of the great American poet and scholar Henry Wadsworth Longfellow and his family. The dwelling was known as the Craigie House in honor of its longtime landlady, Elizabeth Craigie, who rented rooms to many of its famous tenants, including Longfellow.

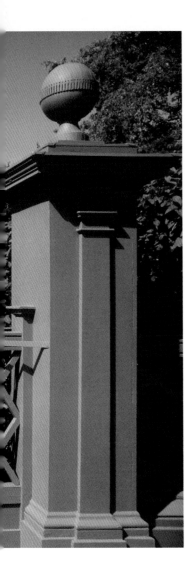

refer to those who were in favor of continued loyalty toward Great Britain.)

But there was no escaping history. As Massachusetts and the other colonies moved into open rebellion, the Sons of Liberty and other rebel groups began taking stronger measures against Tories. In 1774, Vassall and his family were driven from their Cambridge property, which was confiscated by the rebels. The house was put to use in the rebel cause to quarter a local militia group.

Then, in April 1775, the minutemen (as the members of the militia were referred to, supposedly because it took them no more than a minute to get ready for combat) who were alerted by the heroic silversmith Paul Revere and his friends, clashed with British troops at the villages of Concord and Lexington, nearby to the west.

The American Revolution had begun. In July 1775, George

To the right of the stairway in the front hall of the Craigie House is the bust of George Washington. It was kept there by Longfellow in honor of his home's famous history. The bust is a copy of the famous original made by the great French sculptor of the Enlightenment Jean-Antoine Houdon. "The Craigie House is decidedly conservative [old-fashioned]," Longfellow wrote in his journal, "and will remain as much in its old state as comfort permits."

Washington of Virginia arrived in Cambridge on horseback to take control of the motley regiments of rebel soldiers. These regiments had pinned the proud British army down within the city of Boston and were laying siege to the city. The Continental army was born.

Washington needed a headquarters, and the Vassall house was perfect for the new commander in chief. He soon brought his wife, Martha, to the home with him, along with Martha's daughter and son-in-law. Over the next nine months, some of the most famous figures of the American Revolution visited Washington's headquarters in Cambridge—John Adams and his wife, Abigail, John Jay, Alexander Hamilton, Paul Revere, the future traitor Benedict Arnold, generals Nathanael Greene and Henry Knox, and others. For nine months, Washington made the house in Cambridge his headquarters while drilling the Continental army into shape. Finally, the rebel cannon mounted in the hills overlooking Boston forced the British to evacuate.

## KEEPING COMPANY WITH AMERICA'S BELOVED POET

In July 1861, a poet lived in the house, in company with all that history. Not a poet, but *the* poet—Henry Wadsworth Longfellow, the best-known and best-selling American author of his day. He resided there with his adored wife and their five beloved children. For many years the distinguished professor of modern languages at nearby Harvard University, Longfellow was also the author, most famously, of the epic narrative poems *Evangeline* and *The Song of Hiawatha*. He was also known for shorter works such as "The Village Blacksmith," "A Psalm of Life," "The Children's Hour," "The Wreck of the Hesperus," and "The Building of the Ship."

His poems took scenes from everyday American life, or more heroic doings from troubled times in American history, or legendary endeavors from the vast trove of folklore on the American land. He then spun them into the stuff of literature. The publication of each new volume of verse from the pen of

Surrounded by his manuscripts, the poet contemplates meter and rhyme in his study. His study was also where he greeted the endless stream of visitors, famous and unknown, who came to see him in residence. By the 1860s, when Longfellow was the most widely read poet in English, he was considered to be as much of a "landmark" as the Craigie House.

Henry Wadsworth Longfellow was a major literary occasion, both in the United States and in England. The first print runs of such volumes usually sold out within days.

It was as if Longfellow were the storyteller, the bard, who could make the American experience come thrillingly alive for his readers. It seemed as if he somehow lived inside that history: it was well known that he attempted to preserve his home, as much as was practical and possible, to the way it had been when Washington lived there. A marble bust of Washington was the very first thing that greeted a visitor in the entry hallway. One of the poet's most treasured possessions was a lock of Washington's hair that had been handed down in the Longfellow family as an heirloom.

But it was with words that Longfellow honored the American experience. His work made him not so much famous as beloved. Each day, visitors, invited or not, flocked to his Cambridge home near the Charles River. Some were famous, including his friends Ralph Waldo Emerson, Louis Agassiz, Charles Sumner, Nathaniel Hawthorne, fellow poets Oliver Wendell Holmes and James Russell Lowell, and the great English author Charles Dickens. Important literary figures from other countries, such as the British novelists Anthony Trollope, Wilkie Collins, and, in later years, the scandalous Irish playwright and poet Oscar Wilde, came by to pay their respects. The emperor of Brazil, while visiting the United States, asked to be invited over to dinner. He expressed the desire that Emerson, Holmes, and Lowell be present at the same time. Having escaped from imprisonment in Siberia by trekking the length of Asia, then sailing the Pacific, and making his way overland from California across the vast breadth of North America, the Russian revolutionary and anarchist Mikhail Bakunin stopped in one day and stayed for lunch and dinner.

More numerous and frequent were the visits from Longfellow's fellow citizens. The famous and the footloose,

Oscar Wilde visited Longfellow at the Craigie House shortly before the American poet's death in 1882. At the time, although Wilde had not yet penned the works that would gain him literary immortality, he was already an international celebrity for his wit and flamboyance. Although often impertinent to older literary figures, Wilde said of Longfellow after his visit, "Longfellow was himself a beautiful poem, more beautiful than anything he ever wrote."

the anonymous and the anointed, the proud and the penniless all dropped in. They sought everything from an audience with greatness, literary advice, an autograph, and words of wisdom to a free meal. Eternally patient, soft-spoken, and gracious, Longfellow greeted them all, ushering them into his spacious combined study and library at the rear of the first floor. When asked by his friend Charles Eliot Norton, the famed literary scholar, why he allowed his time to be taken up by such people, Longfellow replied, "Why Charles, who will be kind to [them] if I am not?"

## TRAGEDY BEFALLS THE LONGFELLOW HOUSE

In July 1861, the country was three months at war, not with a foreign invader or enemy but with itself. The moment of crisis that so many, including Longfellow, had dreaded for so long had at last arrived. The simmering confrontation between the North and the South over slavery had played out in many different ways over the past several decades. It finally erupted into war with the election of Abraham Lincoln as president and the secession of the Southern states.

A pall of uncertainty seemed to hang over the country, over the Longfellow house, and over Longfellow himself. "If only one could foresee one's fate," Longfellow wrote in his journal on June 19. He was troubled over what the future held for both his country and his family. An abolitionist, although not an

Mikhail Bakunin was among the more unusual of those who made the pilgrimage to see Longfellow at the Craigie House. Born a Russian aristocrat, Bakunin dedicated his life to inciting a Socialist revolution in Europe, which earned him expulsion from France, a death sentence in Germany, and a life sentence in his native Russia. Beginning with God, Bakunin rejected all authority except the individual. After his visit, Longfellow described Bakunin as "a giant of a man, with a most seething, ardent temperament."

activist, he believed the Civil War to be a necessary evil. War is "an infernal thing," he confided in his journal. He believed nonetheless "It is now too late to put the fire out. We must let it burn out." Even so, he was consumed with anxiety about his eldest son, Charles, then aged seventeen. Longfellow correctly sensed that Charles was determined to enlist in the Union forces. For perhaps the first time in his life, he doubted the importance of literature. "When the times have such a gunpowder flavor," he wrote in his journal, "all literature loses its taste."

Friends sensed something hanging over the Longfellow house as well. While riding in a carriage in the neighborhood in early July, Oliver Wendell Holmes confided to another friend that he felt a strange sense of foreboding while looking at Longfellow's home. Just looking at the house caused him to tremble, Holmes said, "for those who lived there had their happiness so perfect that no change, of all the changes which must come to them, could fail to be for the worse."

It was in the quiet of the afternoon on a warm July 9, that lazy, relaxed "pause in the day's occupations / That is known as the Children's Hour," as Longfellow characterized it in his poem of the same name, when his daughters would sneak up on him, climb on him, and playfully pull his hair. A doting father, Longfellow was dozing in an armchair near the fireplace in his study while his children played nearby. In the library, Longfellow's wife, Fanny, was cutting the hair of their two youngest daughters, Edith, aged seven, and Annie Allegra,

This head-and-shoulders portrait of Fanny Appleton Longfellow, the poet's second wife, was completed sometime between 1850 and 1860. On April 7, 1847, while giving birth to their third child, Fanny became the first woman in the United States to be given an anesthetic during childbirth. This was considered a radical medical experiment at the time; afterward, Fanny proclaimed it to be "the greatest blessing of this age."

aged five. Fanny was planning to preserve a lock of hair from each girl by using wax to seal it into a small paper packet. This was a common practice in the nineteenth century, a time in the United States when common diseases carried off many children before they reached adulthood.

In preparation, Fanny had matches and candles at the ready. (The wax used for the seal was first melted over a candle, then applied to the packet and allowed to harden to form the seal.) Somehow—no one is sure exactly what happened—a match or candle ignited one of the folds of her long, flowing cotton dress, instantly setting the entire garment ablaze. In seconds, Fanny was engulfed in flames. Managing to keep her composure, she made it to the library and called to her husband for help. The poet leapt up, trying to smother the flames with a rug and, when that failed, enveloping her in a bear hug.

Eventually, he succeeded, but the damage done had been tremendous. Fanny had been badly burned over much of her body. She lingered for two days before dying from her injuries. She was buried on July 13, the anniversary of her marriage to Longfellow. Very badly burned himself, Longfellow was unable to attend the burial.

## "The Cross of Snow"

The sense of loss that Longfellow felt upon Fanny's death is impossible to measure. His first thoughts were for his children. "My heart aches and bleeds for the poor children," he wrote in a letter to his sister Mary that same month. "To lose such a mother . . . They do not know how great this loss is, but I do." He rarely spoke of his loss to friends but later confessed to one that with Fanny's death, his own life "crumbled away like sand."

Some indication of how much the loss affected Longfellow is evident in how long it took him before he could bear to address it in his poetry. Normally, Longfellow wrote incessantly and quickly, but it would be eighteen years before he could turn his poetic gifts to the death of his wife, and even then he would not allow them to be published in his own lifetime.

A more visible symbol of his sorrow was evident in Longfellow's appearance after Fanny's death. Longfellow's face had been badly burned in the accident, leaving the skin there too tender for him to shave. His beard came in long, full, and snowy white, the same color that his grief turned the hair on top of his head.

To those who continued to flock to Longfellow's home in the years following Fanny's death, his snowy countenance seemed only to add to his poetic aura. They spoke of the "White Longfellow," whose "air of immovable serenity," in the words of his friend Thomas Wentworth Higginson, indicated one who had "learned to condone all human sins." Perhaps only those closest to him realized that the snowy locks hid deep scars.

By the standard of his most famous works, the poem Longfellow finally wrote about Fanny's death, entitled "The Cross of Snow," is, at just fourteen lines, exceedingly brief. None of his works contain as much feeling so beautifully expressed. He begins by speaking of all the "long, sleepless watches of the night" he has spent since her death, staring at her portrait on the wall of the bedroom where she died. "There is a mountain in the West," he then writes, that "displays a cross of snow" in "its deep ravines." "Such is the cross I wear upon my breast," he writes, a symbolic burden of grief that has remained "changeless since the day she died."

"With me all deep feelings are silent ones," Longfellow had written in his youth. It is a strange sentiment for a poet to express, and one demonstrably untrue, no matter how reticent he might have been about expressing his grief. Written on the eighteenth anniversary of Fanny's death, "The Cross of Snow" speaks plainly the language of a sorrow so deep that it is almost inexpressible, telling what Longfellow once called the "heart's deep history."

# CHAPTER
# 2

# THE THOUGHTS OF YOUTH

H enry Wadsworth Longfellow was born in the sea-
port town of Portland, in what is now the state
of Maine, on February 27, 1807. (Maine would
not become a state until 1820. At the time of Longfellow's
birth, Maine was still legally part of the state of
Massachusetts.) He was from solid, respectable Yankee
(as the inhabitants of New England were referred to)
stock on both sides of his family, and his American roots
ran deep. This heritage would be both a foundation and
a subject of his life's work. Secure in his own roots,
Longfellow could confidently embark on the task of
using literature to create an American national identity.

The poet in his prime: this daguerreotype (an early type of photograph) of Longfellow dates from 1848. At the time it was made, Longfellow was still earning his living as a college professor, having, as a young man, deferred his dream of a full-time literary career in honor of his father's wishes.

At the same time, he could introduce Americans to important literature from foreign lands.

## An American Heritage

Henry's father, Stephen Longfellow, was the fourth generation of Stephen Longfellows in Maine. The first Stephen was a prosperous farmer and blacksmith who was also known as a fierce fighter in the Maine settlers' frequent wars with the Native American population of the region. His son, the second Stephen Longfellow, established the family tradition of graduating from Harvard University, in Cambridge, Massachusetts. He served the town of Falmouth, as Portland was then known, in a variety of capacities. These included town clerk, parish clerk, court clerk, notary public, and justice of the peace. A stout, humorous fellow who weighed in at 245 pounds (111 kilograms), he was also known, like his father before him, for his enmity toward Native Americans. He once personally raised the bounty for a scalping expedition against the Indians.

The third Stephen, Henry's grandfather, was also a Harvard graduate. He spent most of his days at the Longfellow farm at Gorham, a small village in the countryside west of Portland. There, he earned his living as a surveyor while winning election many times as a representative in the Massachusetts legislature and as a local judge. His son, the fourth Stephen, likewise graduated with honors from Harvard, but Henry's

The Wadsworth-Longfellow House, as this structure in Portland, Maine, is now known, was referred to as the "Old Original" by the members of the family during Longfellow's childhood. The house was built by General Peleg Wadsworth between 1785 and 1786; he and his wife, Elizabeth, raised ten children there before permanently retiring to Wadsworth Hall on the family farm in Hiram, Maine, in 1807.

father opted to pursue a career in law. Town life being more conducive to a legal practice, he settled in Portland, which was then, as now, the largest town in Maine. There he had a most prosperous legal career and a distinguished political one, winning elections to the Massachusetts legislature, the U.S. Congress, and the Maine legislature.

Zilpah Wadsworth, Henry's mother, was the daughter of a family considered even more distinguished than the Longfellows, and much more colorful. The Longfellows had a history of reliable public service to their community, but the Wadsworths had a family legacy of heroism in service to their country. Also a Harvard graduate, Zilpah's father, Peleg Wadsworth, was a general in the Continental army during the American Revolution. While serving as military commander of the Maine District, he was wounded and captured by the British. He then made a daring and improbable escape that became the stuff of local and family legend. Following the war, he made a fortune in real estate, purchasing nearly 8,000 acres (3,237 hectares) of wilderness land some 50 miles (80 kilometers) west of Portland, which he transformed into a remote, secluded estate. He also established himself as a merchant in Portland, trading primarily in hogs, flour, and firewood and

Even as an adult, Longfellow often visited his childhood home. He wrote his poem "The Rainy Day" at this desk there during a visit in 1841. Childhood memories inspired many of Longfellow's poems. In the poem "My Lost Youth," he wrote of Portland, "And with joy that is almost pain / My heart goes back to wander there / And among the dreams of the days that were, / I find my lost youth there."

still somehow finding time to win the elections to seven terms in the U.S. Congress.

Zilpah Wadsworth and Stephen Longfellow were married on New Year's Day, 1804, in the "Old Original," the luxurious brick home—the first one in town—that Peleg had built near the Portland waterfront. Henry was their second child and second son; to his older brother, born two years before him, went the honor of becoming the fifth Stephen Longfellow. Henry instead was named after Zilpah's favorite brother, Henry Wadsworth, another military hero. As a young officer in the fledgling U.S. Navy, Henry Wadsworth had been killed in 1804 in combat with the Barbary pirates of Tripoli. He and the other members of his crew had decided to blow up their ship rather than accept capture by the pirates.

## CHILDHOOD DAYS

The young Henry Wadsworth Longfellow was close to both of his parents. Although he would not always take it, he would look to his practical, business-minded father for advice throughout his life. According to family members, his artistic inclinations came from his mother, who was "romantic and imaginative" and extremely fond of poetry and music. Her many surviving letters reveal her to be a gifted writer.

The town of Portland also exerted a powerful influence on the boy. He grew up in the Old Original, which allowed him

This illustration of Bowdoin College was completed in 1821, the year of the college's founding. "Bowdoin," said the college's first president, the Reverend Joseph McKeen, during his inaugural address, is "founded and endowed for the common good, and not for the private advantage of those [who come here.]"

to roam the nearby seaside and docks. The sea would be a frequent and powerful image in his poetry, and he was always happiest when making his home within sight of the water. Interestingly, in a time when America was busily expanding westward, Longfellow never showed any interest in traveling inland. He remained instead on or along the Atlantic seaboard his entire life. When he did travel, it was on the Atlantic, eastward, to Europe. As an adult, Longfellow often returned to Portland. He would write about Portland in several poems, calling it in "My Lost Youth," the best known of these works, "the beautiful town / That is seated by the sea."

He would be remembered by family members and friends as a quiet, handsome, obedient boy. He was interested in the usual Maine boys' pastimes–swimming, kite flying, playing ball, ice skating, and so on. He was unusual only with a certain

Washington Irving was one of the first great literary figures of the United States and was Longfellow's first literary inspiration. Born in New York City in 1783, he was named after George Washington, whose biography he would later write. Besides his success as a writer, Irving was also a merchant, lawyer, and diplomat. He also served for fourteen years as the first president of what would become the New York Public Library.

dreamy, distracted quality and his intense interest in reading and books. His father maintained a library of the books considered essential to the education and development of a well-bred young man of the time. The library included collections of the works of the English playwright William Shakespeare, the poets Alexander Pope and John Dryden, the philosopher

Franklin Pierce, who would go on to become the fourteenth president of the United States, was a classmate of Longfellow's at Bowdoin. However, the two were apparently not well acquainted at that time. Upon his election to the presidency in 1852, Pierce became the youngest man to be elected president up to that time. He is also the only president not to swear the oath of office upon his inauguration; for religious reasons, he chose to affirm rather than swear the oath.

David Hume, the historian Edward Gibbon, and the Greek biographer Plutarch. Longfellow read widely in these.

His favorite book, however, was by an American author. *The Sketch-Book of Geoffrey Crayon, Gent.*, by Washington Irving, was published in 1819, and Longfellow appears to have been among its first readers. One of the first genuine American literary successes, *The Sketch-Book* contained two tales that remain well known to the present day: "The Legend of Sleepy Hollow" and "Rip Van Winkle." "Every reader has his first book," Longfellow would later write, in an 1859 essay "Remarks Upon the Death of Irving," "I mean to say one book among all others which in early youth first fascinates his imagination, and at once excites and satisfies the desires of his mind. To me, this first book was *The Sketch-Book* of Washington Irving."

## THE YOUNG POET

"The thoughts of youth are long, long thoughts," Longfellow would write in "My Lost Youth." He was already thinking very far ahead, deciding to become a poet and beginning to develop his artistic abilities at a very young age. Indeed, he became a published poet in 1820, at the age of thirteen. The *Portland Gazette*, a local newspaper, published "The Battle of Lovell's Pond," a poem he had written about a fight with the Native Americans in 1725 in which his ancestors had participated.

Although he did not know Longfellow well at Bowdoin, Nathaniel Hawthorne later became one of Longfellow's closest friends. As the author of such works as *The Scarlet Letter* and *Twice-Told Tales*, Hawthorne became, with Longfellow, one of the most important founding voices of American literature. Hawthorne was melancholy and extremely shy; Longfellow initially found him to be a "strange owl" but ultimately concluded that he was a "grand fellow" who wrote with a "wizard hand."

Longfellow was educated as a youth at home and private academies in Portland. As a young man of fourteen, Longfellow, with his older brother Stephen, was sent off to college. Their father, of course, was extremely proud of the Harvard tradition in his family. Yet he was equally proud of his home state of Maine, newly admitted to the Union in 1820. Accordingly, he decided that his two sons would enroll at Bowdoin, the college established in Brunswick, 30 miles (48 km) northeast of Portland, in 1802. Bowdoin was the first college established in Maine, and the state's most prominent citizens were eager for it to develop a first-rate reputation. Both Longfellow's father and grandfather served on Bowdoin's governing board.

Longfellow spent three years at Bowdoin. Somehow, at the small college with a student body of little more than 100, he managed to avoid developing an acquaintance with two of his distinguished schoolmates. Nathaniel Hawthorne would go on to become America's first great literary novelist and would later become a close friend. Franklin Pierce would become the fourteenth president of the United States. Longfellow did, however, demonstrate a rare ability to learn foreign languages.

Even so, he remained obsessed with literature. He continued to write and sell poems, which were published frequently in literary journals in Philadelphia and Boston. These cities were the literary centers of the United States at the time. As he approached his graduation in 1824, he outlined his future ambitions in a letter to his father. "I most eagerly aspire after future eminence in literature," he explained. "My whole soul burns most ardently for it, and every earthly thought centers on it."

At the time, Longfellow viewed writing as the best means of gaining his own measure of recognition, honor, and distinction in the tradition established by his distinguished family, albeit in a vocation all his own. "I will be eminent in something," he explained in a letter to his father, and he thought that literature offered him the best chance. "Surely," he wrote, "there never was a better opportunity offered for the exertion of literary talent in our own country than is now offered." Stephen Longfellow, however, had a different path in mind.

# CHAPTER 3

# SCHOLAR OF LANGUAGES

Though Henry was the family's second son, he now bore his father's hopes for carrying on family traditions. At Bowdoin, Stephen had shown signs of becoming, as his father had long feared, an incorrigible wastrel. Their father now wanted Henry to follow him into law and was dead set against literature as a proper career for a Longfellow. Writing and publishing poems as a pastime could be considered respectable and even genteel, but the pursuit of a full-time literary career was almost regarded as scandalous.

Father and son were equally determined to get their own way. Fortunately, a compromise soon emerged. In

As captured in this 1824 painting, the marketplace in the German city of Munich was a lively scene. Longfellow's interest in Germany, the German language, and especially in modern German writers such as Goethe put him on the cutting edge of American scholarship in the late 1820s. According to the Longfellow scholar Newton Arvin, "For half a century and more . . . the literature of Germany had been among the richest, perhaps the richest, in Europe; and Longfellow, like no American writer before him, steeped himself in it."

his last semester at Bowdoin, Henry impressed an influential trustee there with the skill with which he translated an ode by the first-century BC poet Horace from its original Latin. Determined to make its mark as an educational institution, Bowdoin was considering establishing a professorship of modern languages. It would be only the fourth college in the country to do so. At the time, only the study of the classical languages—Greek and Latin—was considered essential for a first-rate education. The study of modern languages, which included the European languages of German, French, Spanish, and Italian, was considered to be frivolous by comparison. In his home state, however, Thomas Jefferson had convinced the University of Virginia and the College of William and Mary to make modern languages part of the curriculum. Harvard had done so as well.

## RESTLESSNESS AT BOWDOIN

Their example was good enough for Bowdoin. Impressed by Longfellow's skill with Latin, Bowdoin offered him the chance to become their first professor of modern languages. This was provided he first spent time in Europe learning the languages he was supposed to teach. The prospect of a European tour appealed to both Longfellow and his father. His father agreed to fund it because he regarded a professorship as a much more acceptable career than poetry.

Longfellow was to spend about three years "studying" in Europe, from the spring of 1826 to the spring of 1829, first in France, then in Spain, Italy, and, finally, Germany.

He would always regard this period as a special time. It expanded his intellectual and literary horizons while reinforcing his belief in the possibilities of an American literature. At his graduation from Bowdoin, Longfellow had been chosen to give one of the commencement speeches. In it, he lamented that "as yet we can boast of nothing farther than a first

As it had been for centuries, London Bridge in 1835, the year of Longfellow's second European voyage, was a bustling, chaotic snarl of traffic and commerce. The size and scale of London overwhelmed the American. "It is astonishing how little can be accomplished here in a day! . . . The distances from point to point are so great—London is on so vast and magnificent a scale," Longfellow explained in a letter home to his father.

beginning of a national literature: a literature associated and linked . . . with our institutions, our manners, our customs—in a word, with all that has helped to form whatever there is peculiar to us, and to the land in which we live." Studying the modern European languages in their native lands, seeing the ways in which literature in these languages derived from the particular culture and history of these places, only served to reinforce Longfellow's beliefs in the possibility of an American literature.

Though Longfellow's method of studying was unconventional—he believed that the best way to learn a language was to speak and read it as much as possible through daily interaction with the people of a country, rather than by taking classes in it—he returned from Europe qualified to take up the position at Bowdoin. He found the professorship mostly dissatisfying, however. Frustrated by the lack of quality materials with

which to teach his classes, he spent much of his time finding, assembling, compiling, and in some cases writing material that could be used as textbooks by his students. He was also required to teach many more classes than he expected. Overall, he complained, his academic responsibilities on a typical day occupied him from six in the morning until midnight. This left him with little time to write poetry, which was ultimately his greatest frustration of all.

More satisfying was his marriage, in September 1831, to Mary Potter, a fellow Portland native, five years younger than he was, whom he had known since childhood. But even married life could not quell his restlessness at Bowdoin. By the time of the publication, in 1833, of his first book, *Outre-Mer* (Overseas), a collection of prose sketches from his time in Europe, he was actively seeking new positions.

## A SECOND VOYAGE TO EUROPE

Opportunity came with the retirement, in 1834, of George Ticknor, the legendary professor of modern languages at

The great Scottish historian Thomas Carlyle was among the literary luminaries Longfellow called on in London. Carlyle believed that the "right History" of the French Revolution would be "the grand Poem of our Time." When Longfellow visited him, Carlyle had recently finished his epic history of the Revolution. He had then given the only version of the manuscript to his friend, the philosopher John Stuart Mill, to read. But Mill somehow allowed his servants to burn it in the fireplace.

Harvard. Reputed to be the most learned man in New England, Ticknor knew and admired Longfellow, who had consulted him before embarking on his trip to Europe in 1826. Now, Ticknor enthusiastically recommended Longfellow to succeed him, and Harvard's president, Josiah Quincy, agreed to give Longfellow the position. This was provided he spend at least an additional year in Europe for "ye purpose of a more perfect attainment of German," as Quincy put it in his offer letter. (In large part because of Ticknor's influence, German was fast becoming the language of serious scholarship in the United States.)

This he was willing, even eager, to do. He sailed for Europe in April 1835, accompanied this time by his wife, Mary, and two of her friends. Although his ultimate destination was Germany, he first stopped and spent time in London. There he met Thomas Carlyle, the great Scottish historian of the French Revolution. He also met the brilliant English mathematician and scientist William Babbage, along with his wife, the equally brilliant Ada, daughter of the notorious British poet Lord Byron.

Of these, his visits with Carlyle were to make the greatest impression on Longfellow. He arrived at a difficult time for Carlyle and his long-suffering, eternally loyal wife, Jane. Just two months earlier, the near-penniless couple had learned that the only copy of Carlyle's *French Revolution*, an epic study that he had spent years writing but had not yet published, had been accidentally destroyed through the carelessness of his best

This is Massachusetts Hall, on the campus of Harvard, as it appeared at the time Longfellow began his professorship at the college. At the time, Harvard did not enjoy the exalted academic reputation that it would later earn. The great American historian Henry Adams wrote of Harvard in the first half of the nineteenth century, "Any other education would have required a serious effort, but no one took Harvard College seriously."

friend. Nonetheless, Carlyle remained undaunted, fanatically dedicated to his work. Longfellow described him in a journal entry on June 2, 1835, as tall and awkward, careless in his dress, and "almost clownish" in his manners. But when he spoke, Longfellow wrote, Carlyle's conversation was "glorious," revealing a "free and original mind."

Of greatest interest to Longfellow was Carlyle's interest in the twin pillars of German Romanticism, Friedrich von Schiller and Johann Wolfgang von Goethe. Both of them were poets, novelists, and playwrights. Jane Carlyle told Longfellow that her husband considered Goethe to be "the greatest man that ever lived; excepting only Jesus Christ." Longfellow's admiration for the German literary master would soon be almost as great. He would become the first to teach Goethe at an American college. He always kept a bust of Goethe on his desk in his Harvard office.

From England, it was on to Sweden and Denmark, where Longfellow developed a fascination with Scandinavian folklore that would later exercise a profound influence on his own poetry. It was there, too, that Mary revealed that she had become pregnant, possibly in the course of the voyage over. Somewhat frail to begin with, and already exhausted from traveling, Mary's pregnancy only made matters worse. In October, in Amsterdam in the Netherlands, she suffered a miscarriage. She continued to grow sicker; in late November, in the Dutch city of Rotterdam, she died. Heartbroken, Longfellow had her body embalmed, sealed in a lead casket, and, with a long letter of explanation and condolence to Mary's father, shipped back to her family in Portland for burial.

Though he continually asked himself, as he recorded in his journal, "Why do I travel? Every hour my heart aches with sadness," Longfellow felt he had no choice but to continue with his journey. He had the stoicism in the face of hardship typical of the native New Englander. He also held the belief that work was the best, and possibly only, cure for heartache. "Let us, then, be up and doing, / With a heart for any fate," was the prescription for dealing with even the most difficult of life's challenges that he offered in "A Psalm of Life." This poem, one of his most famous, was written, according to Longfellow, while he was "rallying from [the] depression" caused by Mary's death. He characterized it as "a voice from my inmost heart."

## THE UNUSUAL PROFESSOR

In the winter of 1836 to 1837, Longfellow was somehow able to muster the will to do the work he needed to do in Germany in order to claim the position at Harvard. Even at Harvard, however, academic life continued to be frustrating. Longfellow expected to function as essentially a department chairman with occasional responsibilities for lectures. However, he found himself, from year to year, responsible for much of the day-to-day instruction in German, French, Italian, and Spanish. As at Bowdoin, his academic responsibilities left him with less time than he would have liked for his own writing.

Even so, he could be an inspiring, if unusual, teacher. Some found his clothes too European, eccentric, and dandified, and his language and manner of speaking too refined and even flowery. Yet none denied his passion for his subject matter. Longfellow regarded his classes as being less forums for imparting to his students the rudiments of grammar, vocabulary, and sentence construction than an opportunity for them to immerse themselves in the culture, especially the important literature, that the language was used to express. So he used Miguel de Cervantes's *Don Quixote* as a text for Spanish, Dante's *Inferno* for Italian, Goethe's *Faust* for German, and Honoré de Balzac's *The Wild Ass's Skin* for French. He mixed into the lectures biographical information and historical background about the authors and works being studied. The study of works such as these, regarded today as classics of the literature of their country, marked some of the first times they had been subjected to serious study in the United States.

Sometimes, too, there would be a special treat for the students. One day in 1838, when Longfellow concluded his soon-to-be famous lecture on Goethe by reading aloud "A Psalm of Life." It was the first time that Longfellow shared this poem, with either an audience or reader. He soon began complaining that he was tired of "teaching boys" when he preferred to be "talking to men through his poetry." However, his commitment and passion usually made his teaching an unforgettable experience for his students, no matter what frustrations he may have been experiencing.

# CHAPTER
# 4

# THE FOREST PRIMEVAL

But as Longfellow had always known, it was as a poet that he would fulfill his destiny. In 1839, he published *Voices of the Night*, his first book of poetry. Although it was a very slim volume, containing just nine new poems, it was an immediate critical and commercial success. The enormously talented and extremely troubled Edgar Allan Poe, who would later prove himself to be no great admirer of Longfellow's work, hailed the opening lines of the first poem in the collection, "Hymn to the Night," as possessing the most "august beauty" of any poem ever written. "A Psalm of Life," meanwhile, made Longfellow instantly famous. Among other things, it was the first of several of his poems to introduce to the English language phrases that have since become so commonplace that they are today derided as clichés. In this case, the phrase was "footprints on the sands of time"; there would be others, including the deathless "ships that pass in the night."

*Voices of the Night* was followed, in 1841, by another collection, *Ballads and Other Poems*. According to a recent Longfellow biographer, Charles Calhoun, "the quickness with which the public not only bought this book but memorized the poems . . . was without parallel in U.S. publishing history." Today, in the United States, poetry is written almost exclusively to be read and experienced as a private intellectual effort, but this was not the case in the mid-nineteenth century. Then, poetry was written to appeal to and to be read by large numbers of readers, to be memorized and shared, almost in the way that songs are today. Longfellow excelled at this kind of verse, with "The Village Blacksmith" and "The Wreck of the Hesperus," from *Ballads and Other Poems*, being excellent examples. Even

This engraving portrays a who's who of Boston's foremost mid-nineteenth century intellectuals, all of whom were members of Longfellow's social circle. From left to right: *(standing)* author Oliver Wendell Holmes, educator Bronson Alcott, diplomat and poet James Russell Lowell, and naturalist Louis Agassiz; *(seated)* poet John Greenleaf Whittier, essayist and philosopher Ralph Waldo Emerson, historian John Lothrop Motley, novelist Nathaniel Hawthorne, and Longfellow.

OLIVER WENDELL HOLMES · A · BRONSON · ALCOTT · JAMES · RUSSELL · LOWELL · LOUIS · AGASSIZ · WHITTIER · RALPH · WALDO · EMERSON · JOHN · LOTHROP · MOTLEY · NATHANIEL · HAWTHORNE · HENRY · W · LONGFELLOW

AUTHORS GROUP

when read silently, the words of these two Longfellow classics seem to sing. One can easily imagine them set to a melody.

## DAYS OF LOVE AND HAPPINESS

Success as a poet ushered in the happiest days Longfellow had known since his childhood. He was now the most popular poet in America, and his fame had spread to England as well. While touring the United States, England's own literary sensation, Charles Dickens, had paid a call on Longfellow in Cambridge, where the two launched a lifelong friendship. Longfellow's most important friendship, which was with Charles Sumner, the abolitionist and orator who would later be elected senator from Massachusetts, was in full flower. Emerson and Hawthorne had pronounced themselves admirers of Longfellow's work and had become friends of his.

Best of all, Longfellow's seemingly hopeless love affair with Frances Appleton had taken a turn for the better. He had met the then nineteen-year-old Appleton, whom friends called Fanny, in Switzerland in 1836, some six months after the death of his wife, Mary. A native of Cambridge, Appleton was traveling through Europe with her family. She knew Longfellow by reputation as the author of *Outre-Mer*. She had assumed that the author of the book, which she had not especially enjoyed, was an old man; upon meeting Longfellow she was not greatly impressed.

The visit of the English novelist Charles Dickens to the United States in 1842 for a lecture tour marked the beginning of a lifelong friendship with Longfellow. After their first meeting, Longfellow described Dickens to his father as a "gay, free, and easy character—a fine bright face; blue eyes, long dark hair, and withal a slight dash of the Dick Swiveller about him." (Dick Swiveller is a character in Dickens's novel *The Old Curiousity Shop*—quick-witted, brave, romantic, and something of a rascal.)

Longfellow, however, seems to have been almost immediately taken with Fanny. Once they were both back in Cambridge, he began wooing her, but he proved to be a clumsy suitor. His idea of courtship was reading aloud German poetry to her. She persistently refused his advances, ridiculing him to her friends as "the Prof." Mockery turned to scorn and fury when he published, in 1839, *Hyperion*, a novel in which she was a thinly disguised character. Shortly thereafter, she broke off all but unavoidable social contact with him. This last in a series of rejections by her made him something of a figure of fun in Cambridge, despite his burgeoning literary reputation. But in the spring of 1843, she let him know that she was now, after seven years, interested in pursuing a relationship. They were married that summer. The marriage, which lasted until Fanny's tragic death by fire in 1861, was by all accounts an extraordinarily happy one that was the envy of their many friends.

As a gift to the couple, Fanny's wealthy father purchased the Craigie House for them to make their home. The house had been named after its eccentric owner and landlady, Elizabeth Craigie, a devotee of the French Enlightenment philosopher Voltaire. Craigie refused to kill even insects in her home because to do so would interfere with their right to life. Longfellow immediately loved the house, which was outside the village of Cambridge, fronting on the Charles River, and had been Washington's headquarters at the outset of the American Revolution. It would be his home, under varying

Two friends pose together. This photograph of Charles Sumner and Longfellow was taken in 1863. Trained as a lawyer, Sumner made a name for himself as an outspoken abolitionist and as one of the founders of the Republican Party. Upon his election as a senator from Massachusetts in 1851, Sumner became the U.S. Senate's most outspoken opponent of slavery.

circumstances, for the rest of his life. More content than he had ever been as an adult, Longfellow was now ready to create his greatest works.

## EVANGELINE

While dining with Hawthorne and mutual friends in the fall of 1846, Longfellow was told a dramatic story relating to the

Emile Bayard's nineteenth-century engraving *The Embarkation of the Acadians* depicts *Le Grand Derangement* (the Great Expulsion). This was when sorrowful Acadians were herded to the ships that took them into exile in 1755. Longfellow wrote his epic poem *Evangeline* about the expulsion only after receiving Hawthorne's assurances that the novelist did not want to explore similar material in his own work.

expulsion of the Acadians from Canada during the 1750s. The Acadians were the French Canadian inhabitants of Nova Scotia, which they called Acadia. As Great Britain wrested control of all of Canada from France during the French and Indian War, they came to suspect the loyalty of the Acadians. Great Britain tried to force them to sign an oath of loyalty to the British crown. When the Acadians refused, their fields, homes, and villages were burned, and thousands of them were loaded onto ships and forced to sail southward along the Atlantic seaboard. Likewise refused haven in Britain's American colonies, many of them wandered for years before dying or finding refuge. The largest surviving remnant of the Acadian community made it to Louisiana, where they became the people known today as Cajuns.

It was against this historical backdrop that Longfellow was told the story of a young Acadian couple

"Fair was she to behold, that maiden of seventeen summers, / Black were her eyes as the berry that grows on the thorn by the wayside, / Black, yet how softly they gleamed beneath the brown shade of her tresses! / Sweet was her breath as the breath of [cattle] that feed in the meadows." Thus Longfellow describes his heroine Evangeline in the beginning of the poem of the same name.

by the Reverend Horace Connolly, a close friend of Hawthorne's. This young couple was deeply in love but not yet married and had been separated in the course of the expulsion. As the story went, the woman spent years searching tirelessly throughout New England for her lost love.

Hawthorne had already heard the story several times from Connolly, who repeatedly urged his friend to use it for one of his novels or stories. But Hawthorne had ultimately declined, on the grounds that "It is not in my vein: there are no strong lights and heavy shadows." According to Connolly's

This is the cover of one of the innumerable editions of *Hiawatha* that has been published since 1855. Longfellow's long, narrative poem was an immediate success. It was the first time that Native American culture and themes were validated and celebrated in American literature: "Sing, O Song of Hiawatha, / Of the happy days that followed, / In the land of the Ojibways, / In the pleasant land and peaceful!"

own account of the dinner, Longfellow "followed my narrative with great attention and apparently very deep interest." Upon its completion, Longfellow immediately asked Hawthorne if he had really determined that he had no interest in using it in his own work. When Hawthorne again declared his disinterest in using the material, Longfellow asked if he might use it as the subject of one of his own poems. Hawthorne agreed. (An essay written years later by Hawthorne's grandson Manning Hawthorne and Longfellow's grandson Henry Wadsworth Longfellow Dana, "The Origin and Development of Longfellow's *Evangeline*," also offers an account of these events.)

According to this essay, Longfellow called it "the best illustration of faithfulness and the constancy of woman that I have ever heard or read." He then transformed this material into his great narrative poem *Evangeline*. In his hands, the story expanded from a tale of Acadia and New England to become a great epic of the entire American continent. Evangeline, as Longfellow named his heroine, followed the trail of Gabriel, her lost love, down the Mississippi River to Louisiana, across the western prairies, and all the way back east before being reunited with Gabriel, briefly, as he lay on his deathbed in a Philadelphia charity hospital, the victim of a cholera epidemic.

Longfellow had never seen the Mississippi, of course, never mind Louisiana or the western plains. In his own country, he had never even been as far as Philadelphia. For background, he read up on the Acadian expulsion and let his imagination

The discoverer of the source of the Mississippi River, geologist Henry Rowe Schoolcraft, was for many years Indian agent for the upper Great Lakes region. He lived for years with the Ojibwa people and married an Ojibwa woman. As a result of his experiences, he wrote more than thirty books on Native American culture. Longfellow relied heavily on Schoolcraft's work while composing *The Song of Hiawatha*.

provide the rest of his details. He was aided in that regard by the arrival, in Boston in December 1846, of John Banvard's incredible diorama of the Mississippi–3 miles (4.8 km) of canvas, painted from life with the aim of giving the viewer some feeling for the scope of the mighty river. "The river comes to me instead of my going to the river," Longfellow recorded in his journal upon seeing Banvard's work. His famous description of Acadia in the poem's opening lines– "This is the forest primeval. The murmuring pines and the hemlocks, / Bearded with moss"–was even less scrupulous with respect to reality, bearing a much closer resemblance to his native Maine than to the landscape of Nova Scotia.

Regardless, *Evangeline*, which was published in 1847, was nothing less than a sensation. "It is impossible [today]," wrote the literary critic Cecil B. Williams in his modern biography of Longfellow, "to imagine or understand the reception given to Longfellow's poem." That reception gave him the financial and artistic security to retire, at last, from his professorship at Harvard in 1854. Retirement, in turn, allowed him the time and energy to complete *The Song of Hiawatha*, his even longer epic poem of the folklore of the Ojibwa Indians. Longfellow knew little about Native American mythology, but he pored through the writings of Henry Schoolcraft, a U.S. Army officer who had lived for years among the Ojibwa, and relied on his imagination and literary gifts for the rest. Published in 1857, *The Song of Hiawatha* sold even more spectacularly than *Evangeline* had. It was the most successful of his works to date. By the end of the 1850s, Longfellow was as famous and successful as any writer in the world, with the possible exception of his friend Charles Dickens.

# CHAPTER 5

# "LISTEN, MY CHILDREN"

As Longfellow's fortunes rose, those of his country were fast reaching a crisis point. The country could no longer contain its differences on the question of slavery. As the 1850s drew to a close, it appeared inevitable that the Union would split. For Longfellow, as for many of his fellow Americans, the crisis had been epitomized by the savage beating given his great friend Charles Sumner on the floor of the U.S. Senate in 1856. Following a two-day speech against the expansion of slavery into "Bloody Kansas," Sumner was attacked from behind by Preston Brooks, a

SOUTHERN CHIVALRY — ARGUMENT versus CLUB'S.

A political cartoon from the day depicts the vicious assault by South Carolina representative Preston Brooks on Massachusetts senator Charles Sumner on the floor of the U.S. Senate on May 22, 1856. The attack made both Brooks and Sumner heroes to their respective constituencies and regions.

representative from South Carolina, as he sat at his desk on the floor of the Senate.

With his feet hopelessly tangled in the legs of the desk, Sumner was unable to defend himself as Brooks beat him mercilessly about the head with a gold-headed cane. Brooks continued to flail savagely even as Sumner collapsed into bloody unconsciousness, critically wounded. While Sumner's injuries kept him from returning to the Senate for three years,

Congress, held hostage by the votes of its Southern members, refused to expel Brooks. The brutal incident convinced Longfellow and many other Northerners that the slavery crisis would ultimately be resolved only by fighting.

With the country moving toward civil war, Longfellow's response, as always, was to pick up his pen and write. One result was the stirring patriotic epic, "Paul Revere's Ride," which was first published in the *Atlantic Monthly* magazine in 1861. With the country about to formally split in two, Longfellow looked back to the outbreak of the American Revolution. Longfellow returned his readers to the time when the colonists had first united for the common goal of independence.

## HISTORY AS POETRY

The basic facts of Paul Revere's ride are known to virtually every young student of American history: Paul Revere was a silversmith, a member of the Sons of Liberty, and a courier for the local Committee of Correspondence. He rode out from Boston on horseback by night to warn the villages of Lexington and Concord. In those towns, the local rebel militia had been mustering weapons, and the rebel leaders John Hancock and Samuel Adams were in hiding. Revere warned them that the regular troops of the British army—the "redcoats"—were on their way from Boston. The legend that Longfellow made of it is more irresistible and even better known:

"Listen, my children, and you shall hear / Of the midnight ride of Paul Revere" begins Longfellow's poem. From there it gallops along on words and rhymes as swift and sure as the steed that carried Revere on his errand. Here is Revere advising his anonymous friend about the famous code they will use involving lanterns in Boston's Old North Church to indicate to Revere how the redcoats are coming—"One, if by land, and two, if by sea"—so that he may set out to warn the villages. Here is Revere, rowing "silently," with "muffled oar," across the Charles River from Boston, in the moonlit shadow of a British man-of-war, "A phantom ship, with each mast and spar / Across the moon like a prison bar"; "meanwhile, his friend, through alley and street / Wanders and watches . . ." for anything that will tell him the redcoats are on the move, then "climb[s] the tower of the Old North Church" and places the lanterns that sends Revere off in "A hurry of hoofs on a village street."

The poem rides with Revere as he races to sound the alarm to "every Middlesex village and farm." The hooves of his horse

This illustration from a 1917 edition of Longfellow's "Paul Revere's Ride" captures precisely the dashing individual heroism that Longfellow sought to convey. "On the eighteenth of April, in Seventy-five; / Hardly a man is now alive / Who remembers that fateful day and year," Longfellow wrote. His poem sought to ensure that the date and Revere's deeds will never be forgotten.

Like his fellow poet and contemporary Walt Whitman, Longfellow revered Abraham Lincoln. In his journal, Longfellow hailed Lincoln's victory in the 1860 presidential election as nothing less than "the redemption of the country. Freedom is triumphant." For his part, Lincoln admired Longfellow's poetry, especially "The Building of the Ship."

race "fearless and fleet," striking sparks from the pebbles along the road. (Middlesex was the Massachusetts county in which Lexington and Concord were located.) "The fate of a nation was riding that night," Longfellow tells us, "And the spark struck out by that steed, in his flight / Kindled the land into flame with its heat."

To further impress upon his readers the urgency of Revere's mission, Longfellow counts out the time that his hero is racing against as he gallops through the moonlight. In the opening of successive stanzas, the poet tells us, "It was one by the village clock . . ."; "It was two by the village clock . . ."; "It was three by the village clock . . . ," referring to a different village and clock every time, repeating the phrase "every Middlesex village and farm" so that it seems the entire countryside must be in rebellion. Finally, Revere's mission successfully completed, we are given credit for knowing what we should about our history, as Longfellow paints his immortal portrait of the loosely organized American militia, without uniforms or commanding officers, improvising their guerrilla-like tactics as the proud and powerful British army marches in from Boston:

> You know the rest. In the books you have read,
> How the British Regulars fired and fled, –
> How the farmers gave them ball for ball,
> From behind each fence and farm-yard wall,
> Chasing the redcoats down the lane,
> Then crossing the fields to emerge again,
> Under the trees at the turn of the road,
> And only pausing to fire and load.

"So through the night rode Paul Revere," the poem's final stanza tells us, his alarm "a cry of defiance and not of fear." More important, Longfellow writes hopefully, Revere's alarm will sound again, whenever–as perhaps at the moment of the poem's publication, with the United States on the verge of dissolving into the Civil War–the nation finds itself in similar danger:

All are architects of Fate,
    Working in these walls of Time,
Some with massive deeds and great,
    Some with ornaments of rhyme.

                    Henry W. Longfellow

Sept. 20. 1878.

For an admirer in 1878, Longfellow wrote out the first four lines of an 1846 poem, "The Builders," and autographed it. Particularly as he grew older and his health more poor, friends both marveled and worried about Longfellow's generosity in terms of the time and energy he gave to admirers.

For, borne on the night-wind of the Past,
Through all our history, to the last,
In the hour of darkness and peril and need,
The people will awaken and listen to hear
The hurrying hoof-beats of that steed,
And the midnight message of Paul Revere.

To this day, it is "Paul Revere's Ride," more than any other single piece of literature or scholarship, that informs the popular

American imagination about the beginnings of the Revolution. The lone rider in the darkness; the put-upon farmers, resisting only when given no choice by the advance of the British regulars; the homespun ingenuity of the lantern code in the Old North Church outwitting the massed power of the British Empire, as represented by the hulking man-of-war in the Charles River. This is the way Americans then and now like to think that it was.

That Longfellow's version was not strictly accurate in many regards was of minimal importance to his readers, who wanted poetry, not history, or perhaps more accurately, history as poetry. Revere rode with at least two other men, whom Longfellow never mentions; no one knows how accurate the bit about the Old North Church really is; and, most important, Revere never even finished his mission, as he was captured by the British. Countless teachers of history have since cautioned their students that the popular version of the Paul Revere story—the one that "everyone" seems to somehow know, even if they have not actually read the Longfellow poem—is not historically accurate. That the legend still needs to be corrected is testimony to Longfellow's achievement, proof that poetry can be as powerful as history, for it was Longfellow who essentially created this legend. As is also true of *Evangeline*, historical truth has proved less important than poetic truth. To the present day, Acadians in Canada and Cajuns in Louisiana have claimed Evangeline as a symbol of their culture.

Among poets, Alfred Lord Tennyson, poet laureate of Great Britain from 1850 to 1892, was one of Longfellow's few equals in terms of renown. Longfellow was a great admirer of Tennyson's work and was even accused by Edgar Allan Poe of committing "most barbarous . . . literary robbery" in lifting themes and methods from Tennyson.

"It is a wonderful gift to be able to stir men like that," a moved Abraham Lincoln said of Longfellow after hearing a recitation of another of his poems from this period, "The Building of the Ship," in which the construction and launching of a new ship becomes a metaphor for the ability of the United States to withstand the crisis that now faced it. Once again, as Longfellow has it, and as the Founding Fathers and many Americans since have liked to believe, nothing less than the hopes of humankind is weighing in the balance. "Thou, too, sail on, O Ship of State!," Longfellow writes. "Sail on, O UNION, strong and great! / Humanity with all its fears / With all the hopes of future years, / Is hanging breathless on thy fate!"

## The "White Longfellow"

But for a time, the ship of state was destined to collapse on the shoals. As the nation plunged into war, Longfellow had to endure his own personal tragedy in the form of the death of his beloved Fanny. Her death left him a broken, though not yet defeated, man. Photographs of the "White Longfellow" show the increasing fatigue and sorrow that now constantly threatened to overtake him. Among the millions of casualties claimed by the Civil War was one in his own family. Charles, Longfellow's eldest son, was a free-spirited, fun-loving young man who liked nothing better than to ride, hunt, sail, or engage in any outdoor activity. Having succeeded, despite his father's wishes, in enlisting in the Union army, Charles was badly wounded near New Hope Church in Virginia in November 1863. Although Charles recovered, the fright took an additional toll on his father.

Longfellow continued to work, of course—he could not have lived without work—but for the most part, his greatest creative efforts were behind him. Sometime not long after the death of Fanny, he had crossed that line that separates the power of maturity from the waning of old age. The great American poet was now old. His last major collection of poems, *Tales of a Wayside Inn*, appeared in three separate volumes between 1863 to 1873. None of the pieces included were as long as *Evangeline* or *The Song of Hiawatha*, and very few could match them in imaginative power. Many works looked backward, to his childhood or other days of his past or to bygone eras of American history. One such popular piece, *The Courtship of Miles Standish*, was set in the Puritan era. Tellingly perhaps, he could never seem to muster the artistic will to directly address the Civil War as a subject. Slowly but surely, the world was passing him by.

The transcendentalist philosopher Ralph Waldo Emerson led the calls for the creation of a distinctly American literature. "I have one foremost satisfaction in reading your books—that I am safe," he wrote to Longfellow in November 1855.

There were still triumphs to come, of course. At home, he busied himself with his poetry and his translation of Dante's *Divine Comedy*, which he had begun after Fanny's death as an intellectual exercise to occupy his time and mind. That project gave rise to the formation of the Dante Club, an informal weekly gathering at Longfellow's home consisting of himself, James Russell Lowell, Charles Eliot Norton, and the young novelist William Dean Howells, as well as occasional invitees. Each week, the group met in Longfellow's study, where they listened respectfully as Longfellow read aloud his latest translated verses in his deep, soothing, mellifluous voice. The group then retired to the dining room for a cold supper washed down with good wine. His complete translation was published in 1867, and soon became a staple in every respectable American library.

It remains, in general, highly regarded, even more so than his poetry. Speaking in 2000, U.S. poet laureate Robert Pinsky, whose own translation of Dante's masterpiece is perhaps the most highly praised modern English-language version, said that Longfellow's translation had been "extremely useful" to him while he was preparing his own work. "Of the dozens of translations in English," Pinsky said, "[Longfellow's] was by far the best as a work of art. It is also quite accurate."

In 1881, Longfellow, Lowell, and Norton officially transformed their informal organization, the Dante Club, into the Dante Society of America. Officially located then, as now, at

A stone bust of Longfellow stands in front of sculptures of characters from his greatest poems, including Hiawatha, Evangeline, and Miles Standish, at the Longfellow National Historic Site in Cambridge, Massachusetts.

Harvard University in Cambridge, the Dante Society of America remains the second-oldest officially constituted organization in the world dedicated to the study of Dante's works. In 2003, the original Dante Club even became the unlikely inspiration for a U.S. bestseller. In a work of historical fiction by Matthew Pearl, also called *The Dante Club*, Longfellow, Lowell, and Oliver Wendell Holmes become embroiled in a murder mystery as they are putting the finishing touches on Longfellow's translation.

As fanciful as the work may seem, it shows that Longfellow still exerts some hold on the American imagination.

## Final Years

As Longfellow's production inevitably slowed, his veneration in the eyes of the public only seemed to increase. From June 1868 to September 1869, he made a last trip to Europe, where he was received with all the respect due an aging literary lion and pioneer. In England, he was awarded degrees from Cambridge and Oxford universities and invited to audiences with Queen Elizabeth and Prime Minister William Gladstone.

The audience with Queen Elizabeth delighted Longfellow, who made it the subject of a much-told anecdote that illustrates his gentle sense of humor, especially about himself. When a humble Longfellow expressed, to the queen, his surprise as to how famous he seemed to be in England, she replied, "O, I assure you, Mr. Longfellow, you are very well known. All my servants read you." Longfellow would then confess to his listener that he sometimes woke up in the night wondering if the queen had been deliberately, if subtly, insulting him.

On the Isle of Wight, in the English Channel, Longfellow stayed for several days with the revered English poet Alfred Lord Tennyson. There, his photograph was taken by Julia Margaret Cameron, one of the first great photographers. In Rome, he spent an evening in deep conversation with Franz

Liszt, the magnificent Romantic composer and pianist. Back in the United States, further evidence of his continued stature as a literary figure came in 1874, when he sold a relatively short poem, "The Hanging of the Crane," to a New York newspaper for $4,000. At the time, it was the largest amount ever paid for the publication of a single poem. His last years were spent, typically, pursuing an incredibly ambitious project: the assembly and publication of a massive anthology of verse and poetry from around the world, including Arab and Asian countries. Entitled *Poems of Places*, the anthology ultimately totaled thirty-one volumes in all.

As Longfellow aged, his genuine gift for friendship and hospitality never deserted him. Until he grew sick in his very last years, friends and strangers alike continued to call daily at the Craigie House, and they were always received with kindness. Those who wrote to the poet were treated with similar generosity.

Among the most momentous of these visits was the one paid him by fellow poet and creator of the American identity Walt Whitman, in 1880. Unlike Longfellow, Whitman had enjoyed little popular success, but his critical reputation would soon exceed Longfellow's. Today it is Whitman who is generally regarded as the most important nineteenth-century poet. Of their visit, Whitman later said that he would always remember Longfellow's "lit-up face and glowing warmth and courtesy, in the modes of what is called the old school."

Americans felt almost as warmly about their national poet. In 1879, 700 schoolchildren from Cambridge contributed dimes to be used to present Longfellow with a wooden armchair made from the famous "spreading chestnut tree" on Brattle Street that he had immortalized in his poem "The Village Blacksmith." The following year, the public schools of Cincinnati, Ohio, celebrated his birthday; the year after his birthday was celebrated in most public schools in America. In Longfellow's last years, a friend recorded, when the poet stepped onto a horse-drawn trolley car, "every man in the vehicle rose as a matter of course to offer a seat, and every head was uncovered" as a sign of respect.

Henry Wadsworth Longfellow died at home on March 24, 1882. Sumner and Hawthorne were dead, but Ralph Waldo Emerson, whose vision of an American literature Longfellow had done so much to fulfill, was among the mourners who came to the Craigie House to pay his respects. As he viewed the poet's body, Emerson, who was himself now very old and nearing death, experienced a moment of confusion. "The gentleman we have just been burying was a sweet and beautiful soul," he said aloud, "but I cannot remember his name."

# TIMELINE

**1807** Henry Wadsworth Longfellow is born in Portland, Maine, on February 27.

**1820** Longfellow publishes first poem in the *Portland Gazette*.

**1821** Longfellow enrolls at Bowdoin College in Portland, Maine.

**1825** Longfellow graduates from Bowdoin.

**1826** Longfellow embarks on a three-year tour of Europe to study languages.

**1829** Longfellow becomes a professor of modern languages at Bowdoin.

**1831** Longfellow marries Mary Potter.

**1833** Longfellow publishes *Outre-Mer*, a collection of prose sketches.

**1834** Longfellow begins his second tour of Europe.

**1835** Mary Potter Longfellow dies on November 29, in Rotterdam, the Netherlands.

**1836** Longfellow becomes a professor of modern languages at Harvard University.

**1837** Longfellow begins his long courtship of Frances Appleton.

**1839** Longfellow publishes *Voices of the Night*, his first collection of poetry.

**1841** Longfellow publishes *Ballads of the Night*, his second collection of poetry, to great acclaim.

**1843** Longfellow marries Frances Appleton.

**1847** Longfellow publishes *Evangeline*, a long narrative poem of Acadian displacement and enduring love.

**1849** Longfellow completes "The Building of the Ship," which comes to be seen as metaphor for the increasing divisions between the North and the South.

**1856** Longfellow's best friend, Senator Charles Sumner of Massachusetts, is brutally caned on the floor of the U.S. Senate.

**1857** Longfellow publishes *The Song of Hiawatha*, a long narrative poem drawing on Native American mythology.

**1861** Longfellow publishes "Paul Revere's Ride"; his second wife, Frances Appleton Longfellow, is burned to death in a household accident.

**1863** Son Charles Appleton Longfellow is wounded while serving in the Union army.

**1863–1873** Longfellow writes three volumes of *Tales of a Wayside Inn*.

**1868** Longfellow embarks on his last tour of Europe.

**1874** Longfellow sells his poem "The Hanging of the Crane" for the largest fee in history up to that time.

**1881** Schools around the United States celebrate Longfellow's birthday.

**1882** Longfellow dies on March 24 at the Craigie House.

# GLOSSARY

**abolitionist**  One who favors ending slavery.

**anarchist**  One who rebels against any authority, established order, or ruling power.

**anthology**  A collection of selected literary pieces, articles, or works of music or art.

**apprenticeship**  A period of learning from one more skilled or knowledgeable in a particular trade or subject.

**aristocracy**  Government by a small privileged class.

**assimilate**  To be absorbed into the cultural traditions of a nation or group.

**august**  Majestically dignified.

**Barbary**  A region of northern Africa north of the Sahara, extending from the Atlantic Ocean to the western border of Egypt.

**bard**  A singer or poet whose works tell of the heroic doings of great individuals.

**benign**  Gracious, favorable, positive.

**burgeoning**  Rapidly growing and expanding; flourishing.

**chattel** Property.

**cholera** A deadly infectious disease that was the cause of several epidemics in the nineteenth-century United States.

**deathless** Immortal.

**digression** A turn away from the main point in a written work or spoken argument.

**diorama** A scientific representation displaying wildlife in its natural surroundings, usually life-size.

**eminence** Fame, renown.

**enclave** A distinct ethnic, cultural, or social unit, usually on foreign territory.

**enmity** Hatred or ill-will.

**epic** A long narrative poem telling the deeds of a legendary or heroic figure.

**footloose** Free to move about because of a lack of ties to any particular place.

**foreboding** Dread of something evil or tragic to come.

**genteel** Of or relating to the aristocracy or upper class.

**heirloom** An object of special or sentimental value passed down within a family from generation to generation.

**immigrant** A person who comes to a country to take up permanent residence.

**imperious** Commanding, domineering, arrogant.

**incorrigible** Incapable of being corrected or punished.

**lionize** To treat as an object of great interest or importance.

**mechanic** As used in the nineteenth-century United States, a skilled worker; artisan.

**mellifluous** Having a rich, smooth flow.

**militia** A local military group called to service in an emergency.

**mores** The moral customs and attitudes of a particular group or nation.

**motley** Consisting of mixed or varied elements.

**pall** An effect of gloom or darkness.

**parlance** A manner of speaking.

**pervade** To spread through every part of.

**polyglot** Characterized by several different languages.

**renaissance** Literally "rebirth"; a period of intense artistic or intellectual activity.

**secession** Formal withdrawal from an organization.

**sentimental** Characterized by an excess of feeling as opposed to reason or thought.

**sluggard** Lazy or inactive.

**sonnet** A form of poem consisting of fourteen lines rhyming in a specific scheme.

**Sons of Liberty** A secret organization in Massachusetts and other colonies that enforced opposition to Great Britain's various revenue acts in the years leading up to the American Revolution.

**stoicism** Indifference to pleasure or pain.

**trove**  A valuable collection.

**veneration**  Respect or awe expressed toward a person
   because of his or her character, achievement, or position.

**vitality**  The ability to live and develop.

**wastrel**  Someone who wastes resources or is self-indulgent.

# FOR MORE
# INFORMATION

The Longfellow House
105 Brattle Street
Cambridge, MA 02138-3407
(617) 876-4491

Maine Historical Society
489 Congress Street
Portland, ME 04101
(207) 774-1822
e-mail: info@mainehistory.org

Massachusetts Historical Society
1154 Boylston Street
Boston, MA 02215-3695
(617) 536-1608

The Paul Revere House
19 North Square
Boston, MA 02113
(617) 523-2338

## WEB SITES

Due to the changing nature of Internet links, the Rosen Publishing Group, Inc., has developed an online list of Web sites related to the subject of this book. This site is updated regularly. Please use the link below to access the list:

http://www.rosenlinks.com/lat/helo

# FOR FURTHER READING

Gale, Robert L. *A Henry Wadsworth Longfellow Companion*. Westport, CT: Greenwood, 2003.

Longfellow, Henry Wadsworth. *Evangeline and Selected Tales and Poems*. New York, NY: Signet, 2005.

Longfellow, Henry Wadsworth. *The Midnight Ride of Paul Revere*. Washington, DC: National Geographic, 2002.

Longfellow, Henry Wadsworth. *The Song of Hiawatha*. Holicong, PA: Wildside Press, 2002.

Lukes, Bonnie L. *Henry Wadsworth Longfellow: America's Beloved Poet*. Greensboro, NC: Morgan Reynolds, 2002.

Taylor, C. J. *Peace Walker: The Legend of Hiawatha and Tekanawita*. Toronto, Canada: Tundra, 2004.

# BIBLIOGRAPHY

Arvin, Newton. *Longfellow: His Life and Work.*
Boston, MA: Little, Brown, 1963.

Calhoun, Charles C. *Longfellow: A Rediscovered Life.*
Boston, MA: Beacon Press, 2004.

Emerson, Ralph Waldo. *Selected Writings of Emerson.*
New York, NY: Modern Library, 1986.

Faragher, John Mack. *A Great and Noble Scheme: The
Tragic Story of the Expulsion of the French Acadians
from Their American Homeland.* New York, NY:
Norton, 2005.

Fischer, David Hackett. *Paul Revere's Ride.* New York, NY:
Oxford University Press, 1995.

Longfellow, Henry Wadsworth. *Evangeline and Selected
Tales and Poems.* New York, NY: Signet, 2005.

Matthiessen, F. O. *American Renaissance: Art and
Expression in the Age of Emerson and Whitman.*
New York, NY: Oxford University Press, 1968.

Reynolds, David S. *Beneath the American Renaissance: The
Subversive Imagination in the Age of Emerson and Melville.*
Cambridge, MA: Harvard University Press, 1989.

Tocqueville, Alexis de. *Democracy in America*. Harvey C. Mansfield and Delba Winthrop, eds. Chicago, IL: University of Chicago Press, 2000.

Williams, Cecil B. *Longfellow*. New York, NY: Twayne, 1964.

# INDEX

Plutarch, 49
Poe, Edgar Allen, 6, 18, 65
*Poems of Places*, 95
poetry
  as a career, 53, 55
  and death of first wife, 63
  and death of second wife, 36
  and history, 81–89
  in the nineteenth century, 53, 66
  purpose of, 19–20
Pope, Alexander, 48
Potter, Mary (first wife), 59, 60, 62, 63
Prescott, William, 19
"Psalm of Life, A," 27, 63, 64, 65–66

**R**

Revere, Paul, 25, 26, 81–87

**S**

Schiller, Friedrich von, 61
Shakespeare, William, 14, 48
slavery, 32, 79, 81
*Song of Hiawatha, The*, 27, 78, 90
Sons of Liberty, 25, 81
Sumner, Charles, 19, 30, 68
  beating of, 79–81

**T**

*Tales of a Wayside Inn*, 90
Tennyson, Alfred Lord, 94
Thoreau, Henry David, 6, 18
Ticknor, George, 59–60
Tocqueville, Alexis de, 13–15
Trollope, Anthony, 30

**U**

United States
  and the "American experience," 11
  and immigrants, 7–10
  insecure about its identity, 6–7, 10
  and literature, 13–20

**V**

"Village Blacksmith, The," 27, 66, 96
*Voices of the Night*, 65, 66

**W**

Wadsworth, Zilpah (mother), 43, 45
Washington, George, 15, 25–27, 29, 70
Whitman, Walt, 6, 18, 95
Wilde, Oscar, 30
"Wreck of the Hesperus, The," 27, 66

## About the Author

Meghan Fitzmaurice is a direct descendant of one of the first great American thinkers—Benjamin Franklin. A graduate of Catholic University in Washington, D.C., she has taught courses on nineteenth-century American literature at various colleges.

## Photo Credits

Cover (portrait), pp. 46, 56–57, 67, 93 © Getty Images; cover (background) © Superstock, Inc./Superstock; pp. 3, 28–29, 40, 48, 61, 72–73, 80 © Bettmann/ Corbis; pp. 8–9 © Museum of the City of New York/Corbis; p. 14 Snark/Art Resource, NY; p. 17 The Newark Museum/Art Resource, NY; p. 22 Digital Image © The Museum of Modern Art/Licensed by Scala/Art Resource, NY; pp. 24–25 © Todd Gipstein/Corbis; pp. 26, 35, 42–43, 44, 47, 71, 77, 82, 84, 88 Library of Congress Prints and Photographs Division; p. 31 Private Collection/ Bridgeman Art Library; p. 33 Bibliotheque Nationale, Paris, France/Bridgeman Art Library; p. 50 The Picture Desk/The Art Archive/National Archives, Washington, DC; p. 54 Picture Desk/The Art Archive/State Museum Munich/ Dagli Orti (A); p. 58 Scottish National Portrait Gallery, Edinburgh, Scotland/ Bridgeman Art Library; p. 69 © Public Record Office, London, Great Britain/ HIP/Art Resource, NY; pp. 74, 86 © North Wind Picture Archives; p. 75 University of Virginia Library; p. 91 National Portrait Gallery, Smithsonian Institution/Art Resource, NY.

**Designer:** Gene Mollica; **Editor:** Leigh Ann Cobb
**Photo Researcher:** Martin A. Levick